# FAMOUS INDIANS
## *A Collection of Short Biographies*

KIVA
PUBLISHING, INC.
Walnut, California

Designed & Printed by ALI Graphic Services, Inc.
Irwindale Ca.
Printed in USA
987654321

Kiva Publishing, Walnut, CA

# FAMOUS INDIANS
## A Collection of Short Biographies

Warriors, statesmen, prophets, and scholars; the firmest of friends and most formidable of foes: there are heroes (and heroines) of many kinds in the often tragic, yet inspiring saga of North American Indians.

Most—but not all—of the Indian personalities whose lives are briefly described here were Chiefs; some of them have become famous around the world. All were leaders in a great struggle to preserve treasured lands and lifeways. With their tribesmen, they are inseparably linked to our country's history from its earliest beginnings through generations of growth.

# FAMOUS INDIANS
## *A Collection of Short Biographies*

# POWHATAN AND POCAHONTAS
## (Powhatan)

WHEN ENGLISH SETTLERS founded Jamestown Colony in 1607, all of what is now Tidewater Virginia was occupied by a confederacy of Algonquin Indian tribes headed by a powerful chief known as Powhatan (his proper name was Wahunsonacock). Although Chief Powhatan could easily have destroyed the entire young colony, he and his people were generally friendly during the pioneers' first difficult years.

Capt. John Smith, the English colony's leader, described Powhatan as a tall, dignified man in his 60s, with a grim suspicious face and a reputation for cruelty to anyone who got in his way.

But Powhatan had a very soft heart for his "dearest daughter," Pocahontas, a girl of about 13 at the time of the English arrival.

Many legends have grown up around Pocahontas. One of the most famous of these tells that when John Smith, having intruded too far on Indian territory, was captured and about to be beheaded at Powhatan's order, Pocahontas saved his life by throwing herself over his body. Then, the story continues, Powhatan, yielding to Pocahontas' pleas, pardoned the English leader and sent him back to Jamestown in peace.

*Wahunsonacock, chief of the Powhatan Confederacy, is being crowned "King Powhatan" by Captain John Smith in this pencil sketch by an anonymous 20th century artist. Photo: Smithsonian Institution.*

In 1609, making a diplomatic effort to maintain the Indians' good will, the English settlers crowned Chief Powhatan king of the territory. Much pomp and ceremony went along with the crowning, but, according to Captain Smith, it was not a complete success. Powhatan was more interested in the gifts which went along with the event than in the crown itself, and was reluctant to bow his head even long enough for the crown to be placed upon it.

*Pocahontas, as visualized by an unknown artist of the 19th century, who portrayed the Powhatan "child of nature" in the romantic style of his own period. Photo: Smithsonian Institution.*

Indian-white relations became less friendly after John Smith's return to England, and promises were broken on both sides. The English intruded upon Indian lands, and the resentful Powhatans captured settlers and made off with colonists' belongings. There were several years of minor warfare.

In 1613, taking advantage of Powhatan's great love for his daughter, the English decoyed Pocahontas onto a British ship which lay at anchor in the Potomac, and carried her off to Jamestown. With so valuable a hostage, the settlers were able to arrange ransom terms: English prisoners and goods were returned, and Pocahontas was restored to her father.

But while she was living among the English at Jamestown, Pocahontas had met John Rolfe, "an honest gentleman and of good behaviour," as records of the time describe him. The two fell in love. After Pocahontas had been converted to Christianity and baptized under the name of "the Lady Rebecca," she and Rolfe were married.

The match was much to the benefit of English colonists, for Powhatan kept peace with them until his death in 1618.

In 1616, Mr. and Mrs. Rolfe and several other Indians accompanied Jamestown Governor Thomas Dale to England, where Pocahontas was received as a princess. She lived happily there until, at about 22, she died of smallpox. Her only son, Thomas Rolfe, returned as a young man to the home of his mother, and later founded one of America's most distinguished families—the Randolphs of Virginia. Several remnant groups, representative of the historic Powhatan Confederacy, are found today in Virginia. Of these, the Pamunkey and Mattaponi are best known.

*Metacomet (King Philip), from a 17th century engraving. Photo: Smithsonian Institution.*

# MASSASOIT AND KING PHILIP (Wampanoag)

URING THEIR FIRST hard years in the New England wilderness, the Pilgrims might not have survived without the help of Massasoit, Chief of the Wampanoags, whose territory included parts of what are now Massachusetts and Rhode Island. In March 1621, a few months after the Mayflower landing, the powerful Massasoit, accompanied by several other chiefs, visited Plymouth colony and in a treaty of peace which followed, gave generous amounts of land to the white men.

As long as he lived Massasoit remained a friend and loyal ally of English colonists. One Pilgrim wrote: "There is now great peace among the Indians themselves, and we, for our part, walk as peaceably in the woods as in the highways of England. We entertain them familiarly in our houses, and they, as friendly, bestow their venison on us."

The Indians shared not only their deer, but their planting and cooking secrets as well. The colonists learned to cultivate corn and to make such delicacies as corn pone, planked shad, baked beans, and roasted clams. In the winter of 1623, when Chief Massasoit was dangerously ill, the grateful Pilgrims helped nurse him back to health. The story goes that Gov. Edward Winslow, the colony's leader, personally carried a nourishing broth through several snowy miles to Massasoit's home near what is now Bristol, R.I.

First clashes between Indians and settlers came from quarrels and misunderstandings over land. In most cases, the New England colonists had honorably paid Indians for land, which they then considered their own. The Indians, however, did not understand such European ideas as exclusive land ownership, and continued to hunt and fish where their ancestors always had. To the English this was trespassing, and trespassing meant arrest, trial, and conviction. Tensions increases! between Indians and settlers.

When Massasoit died in 1661, the English, uneasy over the loss of their most powerful Indian friend, hastened to cultivate the good will of the great chief's two sons. As a mark of esteem, they bestowed English names upon the two young chieftains: Wamsutta, Massasoit's elder son and successor, became "Alexander;" the younger, born Metacomet, was renamed "Philip." When Alexander died suddenly a few months after taking office, young Philip was made Chief of the Wampanoags.

Philip reaffirmed his father's peace treaty, and the colonists, in turn, agreed to stop buying land for 4 years. But within 1 year, white settlers were again moving in on Indian territory, and scattered Indian hostilities grew into rumors of war. In 1671 white authorities summoned Philip to Taunton and demanded new peace measures that included surrender of Indian guns. Philip, although bitterly resentful, agreed to these conditions.

But most of the Indians refused to part with their guns. Philip himself, although publicly acknowledging himself a subject of the English king, had privately spent his first 9 years as Wampanoag chief in preparation for a war to avenge his people's humiliations. By 1674, having recognized that his tribe could not defeat the colonists alone, Philip secretly sent messengers to other tribes: war between the Indians and the white men was inevitable, he told them, if the great Algonquian Nation was to survive.

In January of 1675, the war since known as "King Philip's War" began, when an Indian named John Sassamon was found dead under the ice of a pond near Plymouth. Sassamon, who had been converted to Christianity, spoke English well, and for a time had forsaken his white friends to return to the wilderness as Philip's secretary. His real loyalty, though, remained with the colonists, to whom he betrayed Philip's conspiracy. Three Wampanoags, caught by the English, were convicted as Sassamon's killers and executed. The move infuriated the Wampanoags, who wished to administer their own justice in their own way.

To a messenger sent by Governor Winslow to ask Philip why he planned a war against England, the Indian chief haughtily replied: "Your governor is but a subject of King Charles of England. I shall not treat with a subject. I shall treat of peace only with the King, my brother. When he comes, I am ready."

The following June the war began in earnest. At first Philip and his allies were triumphant: Of 90 colonial towns, 52 were attacked and 12 were completely destroyed. Bands of Nipmucks attacked settlers in western Massachusetts, while Philip's own warriors, allied with Sakonnets, Pocassets, and others, struck villages in the Connecticut River Valley.

Historians generally agree that if the Indian tribes had steadfastly maintained their alliance, they might have wiped out the colonists. In any event, the tide began to turn against Philip, and on August 12, 1676, in a savage battle at Kingston, R.I., his Narragansett warriors were overwhelmed by colonists allied with a group of Mohegans. Some time later, King Philip himself was captured and beheaded. Today, very small groups of Wampanoags still survive in Massachusetts, notably on Cape Cod and on Martha's Vineyard.

# POPÉ (Pueblo)

FOR HUNDREDS OF years before the Spanish colonized the Southwest, Indians had lived along the Rio Grande in what is now New Mexico. They were successful farmers, made handsome pottery, and wove fine cotton cloth. Above all, they were extremely religious. The supernatural influenced everything they did.

In 1598, colonists and priests from Mexico under Don Juan de Onate established among these Indians the first Spanish community in the Southwest. The new settlers called the Indians "Pueblos" (the name by which they have since been known), because of the Indians' remarkable villages of large timber and adobe houses. Onate, the new settlement's governor, had Catholic missions and churches built, and in 1610 established a territorial capital at Santa Fe.

The Pueblos' ancient way of life was soon threatened. Considered subjects of the Spanish crown, Indians were required to pay taxes in the form of cloth, corn, or labor. Their villages were renamed after Catholic saints, and their own ceremonies and religious practices were forbidden.

*View of San Juan Pueblo, from a photograph made in 1879. Home of Pope, leader of the all-Pueblo rebellion, the New Mexico pueblo had changed little in the nearly 200 years following Indian insurrection. Photo: Smithsonian Institution.*

13

But although they gave lip service to Christianity, and pretended to submit to Spanish rule, the resentful Indians continued to follow their own sacred practices in the secrecy of their kivas (underground ceremonial rooms).

In 1675 a leader arose among the Pueblo Indians in the person of Popé, a medicine man from a Tewa Pueblo renamed by the Spanish "San Juan." Popé had been one of several Indians imprisoned by the Spanish under suspicion of witchcraft and the killing of several missionaries, and he bitterly hated the white occupiers. Released from prison, he went into hiding in Taos Pueblo, and there planned and organized an all-Pueblo rebellion. The spirits, he said, had ordered him to bring back the Indians' traditional beliefs and customs.

Runners secretly carried this message to all the Pueblos, and one by one, native towns enthusiastically joined the plot. Every precaution was taken to keep the Spanish from learning of the conspiracy: Popé, suspecting even his own brother-in-law of treachery, had him put to death.

August 13, 1680, was the date set for the attack. Somehow, however, the news leaked out, and Popé's only hope was to strike at once. On August 10, with the force of a long-suppressed hatred, the Indians attacked.

Nearly 500 of the 2,500 Spanish population were killed. About 30 priests were murdered in their missions, their bodies stacked upon the altars. Santa Fe, the Spanish capital, was besieged, and its 1,000 inhabitants took refuge in official buildings for about 10 days. Then, after forcing the Indians to a temporary retreat, they abandoned Santa Fe, and, with the remaining Spanish population of the area, fled to El Paso del Norte (now El Paso, Tex.).

Having driven out the occupiers, the triumphant Popé then set out to erase all traces of them. Everything brought by the "Metal People" was ordered destroyed. Indians who had been baptized as Christians were washed with yucca suds, and use of the Spanish language and all baptismal names was prohibited. In Santa Fe, cattle were herded into churches that had escaped burning. Popé did all he could to restore the old Pueblo way of life.

For a time, Popé was received with great honor as he traveled from Pueblo to Pueblo in ceremonial dress. But his success made him a despot. Hostilities broke out between pro- and anti-Popé Pueblos, and he was deposed. In 1688 he was reelected Pueblo leader, but shortly thereafter, he died.

The Pueblos were masters of their own country for 12 years. In 1692, after brief but brutal fighting, Spanish rule was reinstated under Vargas. There was peace in the Pueblos thereafter. The Spanish remained as occupiers for 150 years longer, but their domination was never again as strong as before.

# JOSEPH BRANT (Mohawk)

URING THE AMERICAN REVOLUTION and the years just preceding it, the most powerful Indian friend British settlers had was Joseph Brant (born "Thayendanegea"), a warrior chief of the Mohawk tribe. His lifetime devotion to the English cause started in 1755 when, only 13 years old, he fought under Sir William Johnson in the Battle of Lake George. Johnson, who became British superintendent of Iroquois tribes in what is now upstate New York, was to play a most significant part in the young Indian's life. He had made friends with the Mohawks, learned their language, and married Molly Brant, young Joseph's sister. Sir William took Brant under his wing, had him educated at a mission school (which later became famous as Dartmouth College), and made him his assistant.

In addition to these duties, Brant, who had joined the Anglican Church, worked at revising the Mohawk prayer book and translated parts of the Bible into the Mohawk language.

By 1775 Brant had become a prominent leader, not only of his own tribe, but of the five others which made up the powerful Iroquois League of Indian Nations. As the Revolution began, he accompanied Guy Johnson, Sir William's nephew, on a trip to England, acting as Johnson's secretary. The Mohawk chief was presented at court, had tea with Boswell, and sat to have his portrait painted by the celebrated and fashionable English artist, Romney.

Brant returned to America completely dedicated to the British side in the Revolution. Although the Iroquois League had declared itself neutral, Brant determined to bring it over to the English. British success in driving Washington out of New York in 1776, and the influence of his sister Molly (now widow of Sir William), helped him persuade the Senecas, Cayugas, and Onondagas to join his Mohawks. Members of the two other League tribes, Oneidas and Tuscaroras, chose the American side or were neutral.

Commissioned as a British officer, Brant led strong bands of combined Tories and Iroquois warriors in border raids and battles up and down the Mohawk Valley, acquiring a reputation for both savage ferocity and fighting skill. He surrendered only in the fall of 1781, when Washington sent General Sullivan and his men into the field, overwhelming English and Indian forces at the Battle of Johnstown, and ending war along the Mohawk.

In 1783, the Revolution at an end, Brant, still commissioned by the British and retained on half pay, was rewarded with a grant of English land along the Grand River in Ontario, where he settled with his Mohawk followers. Other Indians from the Six Nations joined them, and the area became known as the Six Nations Reserve. Brant ruled it in peace until his death in 1807, when his youngest son, John, became chief of the Mohawk tribe.

*Joseph Brant (Thayendanegea). The original of this painting of the famed Mohawk chief hangs in the State House at Philadelphia. Photo: Smithsonian Institution.*

He is buried near a small church which he had built on the Grand River near Brantford, Ontario. A marker reads: "This tomb is erected to the memory of Thayendanegea, or Captain Joseph Brant, principal chief and warrior of the Six Nations Indians, by his fellow subjects, admirers of his fidelity and attachment to the British Crown.

# PONTIAC (Ottawa)

PONTIAC, THE OTTAWA Indian chief who organized one of the greatest alliances of Indians in American history, was born in Ohio around 1720. His domain was the Great Lakes country, occupied by the French until their defeat by the English in Canada in 1760.

Ottawas and other Algonquian tribes of the area had lived peacefully among the French, and intermarried with them. Pontiac was at first inclined to be friendly to the new English occupiers, agreeing to acknowledge King George as an "uncle," if not as a superior. But the Indians soon discovered that the British were quite unlike the generous and easy-going French, regarding them as unwelcome squatters on lands rightfully English. With a decree forbidding them to buy rum, the Indians' grievances intensified until by 1763 the entire district was in turmoil.

Pontiac, who had been impressed by an Indian mystic known as the "Delaware Prophet," determined to lead an all-out campaign to right Indian wrongs. Having sent the war belt of red wampum to Indian tribes from Lake Ontario to the Mississippi River, the Ottawa chief, a powerful and persuasive speaker whose air of command marked him as a leader, called upon the Indians to throw the British out. The French were sure to help the Indian cause, he said, and they could stay. He persuaded the Indians to join a daring conspiracy: all British-held posts were to be attacked simultaneously. Detroit, key post of the Great Lakes forts, was to be the prime target.

The plot was launched on May 7, 1763, when a group of Pontiac's warriors, sawed-off muskets hidden under their blankets, entered Fort Detroit on a pretext. The fort was not captured, for its commander had been warned. Elsewhere, however, the conspiracy was successful.

Within a few months, 9 British forts had been captured, and a 10th abandoned by its occupants. Only Detroit, and Fort Pitt in Pennsylvania, still held. With great difficulty, British forces managed to hold off a combined Indian force of about 900 at Detroit, receiving occasional reinforcements through the water route to the Niagara. The Fort was almost exhausted when help came in October. In a bloody battle, Capt. James Dalyell and 220 men clashed with Pontiac at the head of 400 Ottawas and Chippewas. The Indians were victorious, and Dalyell, captured, was killed. But Detroit was reinforced. Pontiac, too, strengthened his forces, and the siege resumed.

At Fort Pitt, two Scottish regiments relieved the post, which had been under heavy attack by allied Delawares, Mingoes, Shawnees, and Hurons. After heavy losses on both sides, whites forced the Indians to retreat, and Fort Pitt was safe.

*This portrait, believed to be of Pontiac, is attributed to John Mix Stanley, one-time resident of Detroit famed for his paintings of Indians. If genuine, it is the only likeness known of the great Ottawa chief, and is published here for the first time. Photo: Detroit Historical Museum.*

All this time, Pontiac, confident that French help would come, had not known that Great Britain and France had signed a peace treaty in London the February before. When he received a letter from the French commander at Fort de Chartres in Louisiana Territory, Pontiac knew there was no longer any real hope of Indian success. Written in fatherly terms, the letter urged "my French children" to bury the hatchet. The French would not abandon their children, but would supply them from across the Mississippi. Now, the letter concluded, the Indians must live in peace. Pontiac had no choice but to end the siege of Detroit. Although he continued to oppose the British through the fall and winter of 1764–65, his Indian allies rapidly lost the will to fight. One by one, Hurons, Senecas, Ottawas, and other tribes gave up.

In April 1765, Pontiac admitted defeat, and helped British forces to subdue scattered Indian bands. Winning the admiration and respect of the British, he lost much Indian support. By 1768, the man who had inspired the alliance and revolt of the great Algonquian tribes had become the target of their jealousy and hostility. In 1769, a Peoria Indian named Black Dog was assigned by a council of his tribe to murder Pontiac, and on April 20 of that year, in Cahokia, Ill., a stab in the back ended the life of the great Ottawa chief.

# SACAGAWEA (Shoshone)

SO MANY ROMANTIC legends have been inspired by Sacagawea, the Shoshone Indian woman who accompanied Lewis and Clark on much of their epoch-making expedition of 1804 06, that even today her biographers differ in many details.

However, the historic *Journals* of the two explorers, and their later letters, tell us much about the famous "Bird Woman," as her Mandan Indian name may be translated.

One of President Jefferson's major purposes in commissioning Lewis and Clark to explore the newly acquired Louisiana Territory had been the establishing of friendly relations with Indian tribes between St. Louis and the Pacific Ocean. Indian chiefs were to be given Jefferson "peace medals" at these historic first contacts with white men.

In the winter of 1804, some 1,600 miles from their St. Louis starting point, Lewis and Clark arrived in the North Dakota country of the Mandan Indians, where they were befriended by the tribe and spent a peaceful winter. Living among the Mandans were a French Canadian fur trader,

*A Mandan village, as portrayed by artist Carl Bodmer in 1833. It was in such a Mandan settlement that Lewis and Clark met Sacagawea and her husband in the winter of 1804. Photo: Smithsonian Institution.*

21

Toussaint Charbonneau, and his young Indian wife, Sacagawea. When the expedition left Mandan country, the couple went with it: Charbonneau, hired as an interpreter for $25 a month; and Sacagawea, her newborn baby on her back.

It seems likely that Sacagawea's main reason for accompanying the explorers was a longing to see her own Shoshone people again. Five years earlier, at about 12, she had been stolen by Crow Indians, taken far from her Rocky Mountain home, and sold as a slave to the Missouri River Mandans. In time she had again been sold, this time to Charbonneau.

If less than the heroine she has sometimes been pictured to be, Sacagawea was unquestionably of great value to the expedition in her role as peace envoy and intermediary with Indian tribes. Clark said of her—"Sacagawea reconciles all the Indians as to our friendly intentions. A woman with a party of men is a token of peace."

Across the Missouri River, Lewis and Clark were faced with the snow-capped Rocky Mountains. Crossing them would be impossible without horses. Going on ahead, Lewis met a band of Shoshone Indians, and persuaded them to return with him to the expedition.

When she saw the Indian band, say the *Journals*, Sacagawea "danced with extravagant joy." She began sucking her fingers to show that these were her people, among whom she had grown up. A particularly moving episode was the Indian girl's reunion with her brother, who had become chief of the tribe. With the tremendous advantage of Sacagawea's relationship, the explorers were able to barter for 29 fine Shoshone horses, and the journey continued.

Across the Rockies, the party built canoes and followed the Columbia River to the Pacific. The two explorers frequently praised Sacagawea's endurance and fortitude in their Journals. She must have been undemanding as well. Lewis wrote of her: "If she has enough to eat and a few trinkets to wear, I believe she would be perfectly content anywhere."

Sacagawea was among those Indians honored with the prized Jefferson peace medal, evidence of the genuine fondness Lewis and Clark felt for her. After the journey, Clark wrote to Charbonneau: "Your woman who accompanied you that long, dangerous, and fatiguing route to the Pacific Ocean and back deserved a greater reward for her attention and services on that route than we had in our power to give her."

Most historians now believe that Sacagawea died around 1812, at the age of about 24. Several monuments honor her memory. One of the best known is that erected by the Wyoming Historical Landmark Commission on U.S. Highway 287, 2 miles east of what is thought to be her burial place in a Shoshone graveyard.

# TECUMSEH (Shawnee)

TECUMSEH, THE SHAWNEE warrior-statesman widely considered the greatest American Indian leader of all time, was a famed fighter against white settlers while still a young man in the Ohio River country. Warfare with whites was a family tradition: Tecumseh's father, also a chief, had died fighting frontiersmen in 1774 when Tecumseh was a boy of six. Two older brothers later fell in battles with colonial soldiers.

Daring and courageous warrior that he was (his name may be translated as "Shooting Star"), Tecumseh was noted for his humanity. He would not torture prisoners, nor allow his people to follow this widespread practice.

By the 1780s, Tecumseh was acknowledged as the leading Indian statesman of the Ohio area. Profoundly disturbed by the growing menace to Indian lands and life represented by white expansion, he worked out a great plan for his people's future. The only Indian hope, he believed, lay in uniting. He dreamed of a powerful confederation of tribes which would create a great Indian state centered around the Ohio Valley and the Great Lakes.

Tecumseh's surviving brother was a visionary who called himself Tenskwatawa the Prophet. In 1805, Tenskwatawa, who claimed to have had revelations from the spirit world, announced a new dogma to Shawnees and their allies. There must be, he proclaimed, no more intermarriage with whites, and Indians were to abandon all the white man's ways. Only when they returned to the old way of life would Indians find the peace and happiness their ancestors had enjoyed. Indian witchcraft and the white man's firewater were denounced alike.

Tenskwatawa's prophecy named his brother, Tecumseh, as the leader who would unite the Indians and guide their return to traditional ways.

The two brothers established an Indian settlement on the Wabash River, near the mouth of the Tippecanoe. There Tecumseh settled more than 1,000 Shawnees, Delawares, Wyandots, Ottawas, Ojibwas, and Kickapoos as the beginning of his great alliance. Liquor was forbidden in the Indian villages, and tribesmen lived according to ancient patterns.

Tecumseh then traveled across the country, urging Indians from Florida to St. Louis to unite. The Shawnee chief was a magnificent figure whose impact was felt by Indians and non-Indians alike. A white observer of the period who heard him speak reported that Tecumseh's voice "resounded over the multitude . . . hurling out his words like a succession of thunderbolts."

To every American and British leader who would listen Tecumseh argued tirelessly that the U.S. Government had no right to buy land from a single tribe, since the entire Ohio Valley country had belonged to all the tribes in common. His repeated position was that the Treaty of Greenville, made in 1795, had guaranteed the tribes, as one people, all Ohio land which had not specifically been ceded to the whites.

The Northwest Territory's new Governor, William Henry Harrison, was all too conscious of these provisions protecting Indian interests in the Greenville Treaty, and was equally determined to undo them. He and Tecumseh, the area's two outstanding figures, met frequently. Harrison refused to recognize the Shawnee chief's arguments; Tecumseh refused to give up his plan for Indian unity. "It is my determination," he told Governor Harrison, "nor will I give rest to my feet until I have united all the red men."

*Tecumseh in the uniform of a British officer. Uniform, cap, and medal were added to this 1808 pencil sketch after the Shawnee chief was commissioned during the War of 1812. The red cap was ornamented with colored porcupine quills and a single, black eagle feather. Photo: Smithsonian Institution.*

24

Hoping to obtain British help, Tecumseh traveled frequently to Canada. He returned with gifts of ammunition, arms, and clothing from his friends, but could not yet be sure enough of English support, nor of complete Indian cooperation, to risk an open attack.

Meanwhile, Governor Harrison was steadily undermining the Greenville Treaty by making separate agreements with some 11 tribes. He dismissed Tecumseh's protests with the dubious logic that the Shawnees, Tecumseh's own people, had not been involved in these deals. Harrison recognized a formidable adversary in Tecumseh, whom he described in a letter to the Secretary of War as "one of those uncommon geniuses which spring up occasionally to produce revolutions." If the whites were any weaker, Harrison went on to say, Tecumseh might succeed in setting up a great empire within the United States.

In the spring of 1811, while Tecumseh was in the south attempting to persuade Creeks, Choctaws, and Chickasaws to join his alliance, Indians at Tippecanoe launched a series of thefts and other harassments of colonists. Harrison, taking advantage of Tecumseh's absence, sent some 900 soldiers to Tippecanoe.

In disobedience of Tecumseh's explicit instructions, Tenskwatawa ordered the Indians to attack, touching off the Battle of Tippecanoe. At its end, the Indians were defeated, scattered, and disillusioned as well, for they had believed the Prophet's claim that white men's bullets would be made harmless.

Tecumseh returned to find his alliance shattered, his hopes all but destroyed. He went to Canada as the War of 1812 was beginning, and the British, who greatly respected him, made the Shawnee chief a brigadier general. Resplendent in uniform, Tecumseh led white and Indian troops in four major battles against the Americans.

In October, 1814, the British made their last stand in the Battle of the Thames in Ontario. Allied English and Indian forces were completely defeated by Harrison (by then also a brigadier general) and his men. Tecumseh himself fell in the battle, at 45 finally defeated by his old adversary.

Perhaps he had felt the approach of death, for the great leader had changed from army uniform to Indian buckskins before the battle. His body was never found.

# SEQUOYA (Cherokee)

BY THE EARLY 1820s, Cherokee Indians of the southeastern United States had reached a remarkable level of civilization. They were good farmers; owned plows, wagons, and thousands of livestock; they wove their own cloth for clothing; operated sawmills and grist mills, blacksmith shops and ferries; and had built roads, schools, and churches. They governed themselves, with a constitutional system they had patterned after that of the United States.

The tribe's outstanding achievement, in 1821, was the development of a system of writing the Cherokee language. It was the invention of Sequoya, a tribal member sometimes called George Gist.

Sequoya, who had grown up among the Cherokees, had been a hunter and fur trader until permanently crippled in a hunting accident. He had never gone to school, and could neither speak nor understand English. But he was by nature a thoughtful and talented man. Having observed the importance of reading, writing, and printing among whites, he pored over English letters in mission-school primers, and set out to develop a Cherokee alphabet.

Some of his tribesmen, frightened at the strange-looking symbols on which Sequoya was constantly at work, suspected him of witchcraft. His cabin and all his working papers were burned, and Sequoya left Cherokee country for the sake of his great project, settling for a time in Arkansas among those Cherokees who had emigrated west.

Twelve years after he had first dreamed of a Cherokee writing system, Sequoya returned to his people, bringing a written greeting from Cherokees in the west. He had succeeded in inventing an alphabet, made up partly of English characters (but with sounds differing from English) and partly of new ones of his own. The first Indian writing system north of Mexico ever devised without white help, it was a brilliant achievement that revolutionized Cherokee education.

Within a year, thousands of Cherokee Indians of all ages had learned to read and write their own language. Parts of the Bible were printed in Cherokee in 1824, and in 1828, having acquired a a press of their own, the tribe began publication—in Cherokee and English—of a weekly newspaper, The Cherokee *Phoenix*. Sequoya was honored by the Cherokee Legislature with a silver medal and a lifetime pension, the first ever given by an Indian tribe.

Sequoya lived among the Arkansas Cherokees as a leader and teacher until 1842, when his thirst for knowledge led him on another search. This time he hoped to find a "lost" band of Cherokees supposed to have crossed the Mississippi many years before, and to look for similarities of speech and grammar among various tribes. He disappeared into the southwest, and was not heard from again.

Three years later, a Cherokee named Oo-no-leh, sent to look for Sequoya, wrote from Mexico City (in the Cherokee language) to the tribe that their most honored leader had died there in 1843.

*Sequoya, the inventor of the Cherokee alphabet, wears the silver medal presented to him by the Cherokee legislature in 1824 to honor his achievement. Photo: Smithsonian Institution.*

# JOHN ROSS (Cherokee)

IN OCTOBER of 1828, a blue-eyed, fair-skinned man stood before the General Council of the Cherokee Indian tribe, raised his right hand, and pledged: "I do solemnly swear that I will faithfully execute the office of Principal Chief of the Cherokee Nation, and will, to the best of my ability, preserve, protect and defend the Constitution of the Cherokee Nation."

John Ross, the man who took the oath of office so much like that of incoming Presidents of the United States, had much white ancestry. But his Scottish immigrant father, while having the boy educated by white teachers, had brought up "Tsan-Usdi" (Little John) as an Indian among Indians. John Ross considered himself a Cherokee, grew up to marry a Cherokee girl, and was to devote his life to leadership of the people he loved.

By the time Ross took his oath as Principal Chief of the new Cherokee Government, the tribe had gone far toward civilization. They were accomplished farmers, cattlemen, and weavers; had built roads, schools, and churches, and, through the invention by their

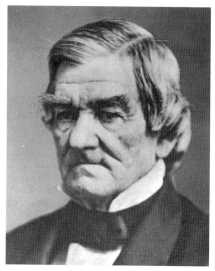

*This 1858 photo of John Ross was made while the Cherokee leader was in Washington, D.C., on tribal business as principal chief of the United Cherokee Nation. Photo: Smithsonian Institution.*

great tribesman Sequoya of a Cherokee alphabet, were largely literate. In 1826 the Cherokee Nation formed a government patterned after that of the United States, its capital at New Echota, Georgia.

John Ross was the logical choice as Principal Chief, for he had been a tribal leader since 1813, when he had fought under General Jackson and his men against the Creeks. As president of the Cherokee National Committee from 1819 to 1826 he had promoted the education and mechanical training of the Indians, and worked in development of the new government.

But the Cherokees' "golden age" was to be a brief one, for as early as 1802 the Federal Government had promised the State of Georgia that Indians would, in time, be removed from their lands. In 1822 the House of Representatives voted to take away Cherokee land titles. To this move the Cherokee Council responded by voting to make no more treaties with the United States. Neither persuasion, threats, nor the bribery attempts of two commissioners, sent to the tribe from Washington, could change Cherokee resistance.

But Georgia continued to maintain that the Indians were only tenants on their lands, and between 1828 and 1831 the Georgia legislature ruthlessly stripped the Cherokees of all their civil rights. When gold was discovered on tribal lands, Cherokee fate was sealed: answering demands of the Georgia legislature, the U.S. Congress appropriated $50,000 for removal of the tribe.

John Ross worked tirelessly in defending the right of Cherokees to their ancestral lands, and headed several delegations to Washington, but without success. His own home was confiscated, and for a time he was imprisoned. The tribal newspaper, the Cherokee *Phoenix,* was suppressed.

In 1835, under the Treaty of New Echota, all Cherokee lands east of the Mississippi were ceded and the tribe was given 2 years to move to Indian Territory (Oklahoma). No official of the Cherokee Nation had been a party to the removal agreement, and some 16,000 Cherokees signed a petition to Washington declaring that their tribesmen had been tricked by white negotiators at New Echota. The petition and all Ross's pleas were ignored by President Jackson.

Although about 2,000 Cherokees had gone west after 1836, the remaining 15,000 stayed on, hopeful that Ross would succeed in his fight. In May, 1838, Gen. Winfield Scott and 7,000 men arrived in Cherokee country and herded the Indians into stockades in preparation for forced removal. The following October they were released, and to Ross fell the sad task of leading his people from their homes.

More than 4,000 Cherokees died of exposure, hunger, and sickness during the terrible 6-month-long trip west. Ross's wife was among them, and the Cherokee leader buried her in Little Rock, Ark. The journey to the West became known among the Cherokees as Nuna-da-ut-sun'y—"The Trail Where They Cried." History records it as "The Trail of Tears."

In Indian Territory the new migrants, joining Cherokee "old settlers," eventually marshaled their forces, formed a new constitution, and at a national Cherokee convention elected John Ross, Principal Chief of the United Cherokee Nation in its new capital at Tahlequah, Okla. Although dissensions caused by the Civil War led the Federal Government to depose him for a time, he was returned to office. The Cherokee chief— statesman to the end—continued to lead his people until he died in 1866, while in Washington working on a treaty to continue the Cherokee Government.

# BLACK HAWK (Sauk)

IN 1804, MEMBERS of the closely related Sauk and Fox Indian tribes were persuaded to surrender to the U.S. Government all their homelands east of the Mississippi River. A provision of the treaty specified that the two tribes would remain undisturbed until white settlement extended to their lands.

For centuries, Sauks and Foxes had hunted and fished in the rich prairie valleys of what are now Illinois and Wisconsin. Most tribesmen knew nothing about the 1804 treaty until, in the 1820's, streams of white settlers pushed into their territory. The immigrants appropriated the Indians' cornfields, plowed among their graves, and began to press for their complete removal.

Indian ranks split into two factions. One was headed by the Sauks' head man, Keokok, who had bowed to the inevitable, cultivated American friendship, and led his followers to new lands in Iowa.

His rival, Black Hawk, a Sauk of the Thunder clan, bitterly opposed the Americans. From boyhood, when his hero had been the legendary Pontiac, Black Hawk had hated white men. His fame as a warrior began at 15, when he killed and scalped his first man. Black Hawk went on to fight, first, enemy Indian tribes, then Americans, throughout the War of 1812.

Above all else, Black Hawk furiously resented the 1804 treaty which had taken away Sauk and Fox lands. He repeatedly denounced it, maintaining that it was invalid since Indian signers had been made drunk and were deceived into agreeing to its terms.

"My reason teaches me that land cannot be sold," Black Hawk was to write in his autobiography many years later. "The Great Spirit gave it to his children to live upon. So long as they occupy and cultivate it they have a right to the soil. Nothing can be sold but such things as can be carried away."

Despite Keokuk's efforts to persuade them, Black Hawk and his followers refused to leave their Illinois villages. By 1831, as the Indians found themselves unable to farm their own lands, Black Hawk ordered whites to get out or be killed. Soldiers and Illinois militia moved in and evicted the Indians.

As Pontiac and Tecumseh had done before him, Black Hawk visualized an Indian confederacy strong enough to withstand the whites. He set out to enlist the support of the Winnebagos, Potawatomies, Foxes and other tribes, while, at the same time, seeking to undermine Keokok, his rival.

In April 1832, Black Hawk with several hundred warriors returned to Illinois prepared to drive out the whites and retake tribal lands, and the fighting known as "Black Hawk's War" began. Only the Foxes had joined Sauks in Black Hawk's confederacy, but it was a dangerous enough threat to force the American Government to put troops into the field. For 3 months the Indians managed to elude the Army, winning several skirmishes and terrorizing the Illinois frontier.

The tide turned as more soldiers poured in, pursuing the Indians across Illinois to the Mississippi. There, trapped between the steamship "Warrior" on one side and the Army on the other, Black Hawk's band was nearly destroyed. The Sauk leader himself escaped to a Winnebago village, surrendered, and was taken in chains to a prison camp. Several months later he was released and sent on a trip to the East which included a visit to President Jackson.

"We did not expect to conquer the whites," the Sauk warrior told the President. "I took up the hatchet to revenge injuries which my people could no longer endure. Had I borne them without striking, my people would have said—'Black Hawk is a woman; he is too old to be a chief; he is no Sauk.'"

*Black Hawk, from a painting by George Catlin, made in 1832 at Jefferson Barracks near St. Louis, Mo., where the Sauk chief was imprisoned at the close of the Black Hawk War. Photo: Smithsonian Institution.*

Black Hawk was received as a hero in several eastern cities, and returned with gifts from American officials. Again in 1837 he traveled to the East, this time with Keokuk.

But, soon thereafter, the old warrior was crushed when President Jackson ordered that Keokuk be made principal chief of the Sauk Nation, which would from then on have only one band instead of two. In 1838, at the age of 71, Black Hawk died in his lodge on the Des Moines River, on the reservation ruled by Keokuk.

In accordance with his request, Black Hawk's body was seated on the ground under a wooden shelter, in old Sauk tradition. He was dressed in the military uniform given him by Jackson and decorated with medals from John Quincy Adams, the President, and the city of Boston. Between his knees was a cane, the gift of statesman Henry Clay.

# OSCEOLA (Creek)

IN 1832 A FEW members of the Seminole tribe of Florida signed an agreement with U.S. Government officials which was to become hated among the Seminoles as the Treaty of Payne's Landing.

Under it, within 3 years the entire tribe would surrender all its Florida lands, move to Indian territory (Oklahoma), and there join members of the Creek tribe. These harsh terms became even more hateful with a later declaration that no Negro would be allowed to accompany the tribe west. For more than 20 years the Seminoles had given refuge to the escaped slaves of both Indian and white owners, had in turn enslaved them and intermarried with them. The no-Negro decree would mean the breaking up of many Seminole families.

Most members of the tribe indignantly repudiated the treaty. As time for removal neared, their resistance to it intensified under the leadership of Osceola, a handsome young Indian of Creek and possibly some European ancestry.

Osceola was less than 30 at the time, and not a chief either by election or inheritance, but was acknowledged as the Seminoles' strong man. He had fully demonstrated his courage and intelligence as a warrior during fights against General Jackson and his men in the First Seminole War (1819). Osceola expressed open contempt for the 1832 treaty and repeatedly refused to sign it, despite pressure from Gen. Wiley Thompson, its chief sponsor.

Continuing his effort to get unanimous Seminole approval, General Thompson called together a group of tribal leaders in 1835. Most of the chiefs who opposed the treaty stood by silently, refusing to take the pen offered them, but Osceola furiously plunged his hunting knife into the paper, declaring that he would never agree to the treaty's terms, and would do all he could to encourage Seminole resistance. Thompson had Osceola arrested, put into irons, and imprisoned.

The wily Osceola quickly got himself released by pretending that he had changed his mind about the treaty and would sign it. As soon as he was free, he began to organize his resistance campaign.

Osceola was too experienced to attempt open battle against the whites' superior military power. Instead, he formed small parties of Indian warriors, instructed them to cause Government forces as much irritation as they could, kill when possible, and then vanish into the wilderness. Women, children, and the old and sick of the tribe were hidden in the depths of the Florida swamps. The leading Seminole signer of the treaty, Charlie Amathla, was killed.

So successful was Osceola's guerrilla warfare that U.S. troops were sent into the field. On Christmas Eve, 1835, more than 100 soldiers under Major Dade set out from the military post at Fort King, confident of capturing the Seminoles' leader. Three days later all but three were dead, having been ambushed and cut down by Osceola and his men. The Indian leader went on to avenge the despised Payne's Landing Treaty by killing General Thompson and four other officers. The Second Seminole War had begun.

For the next 7 years a deadly game of cat and mouse was played in the Florida swamps and Everglades, as the U.S. Army tried to catch Osceola and his people. Immediately after the December massacres, 700 men, sent to bring in the most wanted Indian, faced Osceola and his warriors in the battle of the Ouithlacoochee River. After heavy losses on both sides, the Indians were forced to retreat, but Osceola, although wounded, escaped.

Officer after officer, and more and more troops, went to Florida to bring in the elusive Osceola, who remained invisible. In May of 1837, Gen. T. S. Jesup, latest in a long line of commanders sent to bring the Seminole War to an end, called a peace council attended by Osceola and some 3,000 Indians.

*This portrait of Osceola by George Catlin was made in 1838, just before the handsome young leader of Seminole resistance died while a prisoner at Fort Moulerie, S.C. Photo: Smithsonian Institution.*

Jesup was so sure of success that he had 24 transports standing by, ready to take the Seminoles west. But Osceola got wind of the plot. The next morning, every Indian had vanished.

"No Seminole proves false to his country, nor has a single instance ever occurred of a first-rate warrior having surrendered," wrote the frustrated Jesup. Failing to capture Osceola in battle or through "peacemaking" tactics, Jesup finally succeeding in seizing Osceola only by violating a flag of truce under which the Indian leader was awaiting Jesup for a conference requested by the General. Osceola and a group of his followers were imprisoned in Fort Moultrie, Fla.

The Swamp Fox could not endure captivity, and rapidly wasted away in prison. Within 3 months, in January of 1838, Osceola died.

The Second Seminole War was to go on for 4 more years, as a succession of military leaders declared that the Seminoles could never be defeated. The Indians came out of the swamp only in the fall of 1841, rather than forfeit the lives of a group of their tribesmen, who had been captured and held as hostages. After a peace treaty in 1842, most of the Seminoles moved to Indian territory.

Several bands refused to move. Their descendants (some of whom, although unrelated to the great resistance leader, bear the name "Osceola") are still there, making up today's Seminoles of Florida.

# COCHISE (Apache)

THE WILD CHIRICAHUA Apaches of Arizona territory, although almost constantly battling their traditional enemies, the Mexicans, were not unfriendly to American settlers of the 1850's, and some members of the band even worked for them as woodcutters at the stagecoach station in Apache Pass.

But in 1861, when the child of a settler's family was abducted, Chiricahuas were assumed to be guilty. Six of their chiefs, among them the youthful leader Cochise, were called in for questioning by troops from the 7th Cavalry. A white flag of truce flew over the commander's tent in which they met.

As the Apaches steadfastly denied their guilt and refused to confess to the crime, the commander ordered them seized and arrested. One Chiricahua was killed, and four others were held, but Cochise, cutting through the side of the tent, escaped, three bullets in his body.

Cochise at once began a campaign to avenge his tribesmen, who, following his escape, had been hanged by Federal troops. He directed Apache bands in attacks up and down the territory which were so ferocious that the troops were forced to retreat. For a time Arizona was at the mercy of the triumphant Indians. A territorial newspaper, the *Arizonian*, reported in August 1861: "We are hemmed in on all sides by the unrelenting Apache. Within but 6 months, nine-tenths of the whole male population have been killed off, and every ranch, farm, and mine in the country has been abandoned in consequence."

With the recall of troops from Arizona forts for Civil War duty in the East, the Apaches were convinced that they would succeed in preventing Americans from settling in Apacheland. By the end of 1862, Gen. James Carleton and an army of 3,000 California volunteers marched into southeastern Arizona to put down the Apaches and re-establish communications between the Pacific Coast and the East. Cochise, Mangas Coloradas (a leading Apache chief of the Mimbreño band), and their warriors defended Apache Pass against the Californians until forced to give way before the howitzers of white volunteers.

With the death in prison of Mangas Coloradas "while attempting to escape" the red-hot bayonet of a white soldier, Cochise became principal chief of the Apaches. As troops returned to Arizona territory following the Civil War, an all-out drive to exterminate the Apaches got underway.

Driven into the mountains, Cochise, with not more than 200 warriors, was to hold the U.S. Army at bay for over 10 years. The Apache chief and his men were tough, skillful warriors, constantly alert, and able to vanish as if by magic. Although they were forced deeper and deeper into their mountain hideaways, they continued to carry on guerrilla warfare. White settlements, ranches, and mines were reestablished, but no Apache band was ever captured, and the Chiricahuas' raids

In June of 1871, the famed Indian fighter, Gen. George Crook, took command of the Department of Arizona, under orders to restore peace and law to the territory and subdue the Apaches. Despite his military skill, Crook was a fair and just man who did not believe in exterminating the Indians. He recognized the Apaches' just claims, respected their ability as warriors, and dealt honorably with them. He won their respect in return.

Crook determined to fight fire with fire. Since alliances among Apaches as a whole had never been strong, he was able to win over a good many warriors, whom he then used to fight those who remained hostile. Crook's Apache scouts became famous, and within a few months, most of the Indians had been brought onto reservations. Cochise himself surrendered in September, 1871.

The following spring, resisting transfer to the newly established Tularosa Reservation in New Mexico, Cochise and some 200 followers escaped. But when the Chiricahua Reservation (later discontinued) was established in Arizona in the summer of 1872, he again gave himself up. There the great Apache leader lived peacefully until his death in the summer of 1874. A few hundred Apache "renegades" were still at large. War against them went on until the end of that year, when Crook could claim—for a time—that peace had been restored to Arizona territory.

*Cochise's stronghold in the Dragoon Mountains of Arizona. Such forbidding territory as this helped the Apache leader and his followers to attack and elude the U.S. Army successfully for many years. Photo: Smithsonian Institution.*

# SEATTLE (Suquamish)

THE NAME OF SEATTLE, Suquamish Indian chief, lives on not only in Washington's largest city, but in its State history, which gratefully records him as "the greatest Indian friend white settlers ever had."

Seattle, son of Chief Schweabe, witnessed as a boy the 1792 arrival in Puget Sound of British explorer Vancouver and his men, in their "immense whitewinged bird ship," the Discovery. The wonderful new riches, and the friendliness of the first white men he had ever seen, profoundly impressed Seattle, who became convinced as he grew up that peace, not war, was the right path for all men to follow.

It was a revolutionary belief. Battle and pillaging were a long-established way of life among Pacific Coast Indians, and as a young man, Seattle planned and led an alliance of six tribes against "horse tribes" to the northeast. Although his success in the undertaking won the young chief the high position of "Chief of the Allied Tribes" (the Duwamish Confederacy), it was his last feat as a warrior. Seattle devoted the rest of his life to promoting peace.

When Catholic missionaries entered the Northwest in the 1830's, Seattle became a convert to Christianity and took the baptismal name "Noah," after his favorite Biblical character. He inaugurated regular morning and evening prayers among his people, a practice they continued after his death.

Seattle had ample opportunity to demonstrate his belief in brotherhood. White settlers who founded a small community on Puget Sound in 1851 received unlimited friendship and help from him, and shared his people's fish, seafood, and venison. In 1852, the little settlement which had first been hopefully called "New York," and later "Alki Point," was renamed, for all time, "Seattle."

But as more white immigrants came to the Northwest, relations with the Indians became strained and stormy. During the winter of 1854–55, several northwest tribes organized in the hope of driving whites out of the country. In January 1855, Washington Territory's first Governor and Superintendent of Indian Affairs, Isaac I. Stevens, called Seattle's bands together, and told them of plans for a treaty which would place them on reservations.

Seattle, over 6 feet tall, broad-shouldered, deep-chested, an impressive and powerful orator, replied to the Governor in a resounding voice which all his people assembled along the beach could hear. According to a white spectator's translation, the dignified old leader's words, although marked by sadness and resignation, were poetic. They are said to have gone, in part:

"Whatever I say, the Great Chief at Washington can rely on," Seattle said. "His people are many, like grass that covers vast prairies. Our people once covered the land as waves of a wind-ruffled sea cover its shell-paved floor, but now my people are few.

"Our great and good Father sends us word that if we do as he desires he will buy our lands . . . allow us to live comfortably . . . protect us with his brave warriors; his wonderful ships of war will fill our harbors. Then our ancient northern enemies will cease to frighten our women, children and old men.

"But day and night can not dwell together. The red man has ever fled the approach of the white man as morning mist flees the rising sun. It matters little where we pass the remnant of our days. They will not be many. The Indian's night promises to be dark . . . a few more moons . . . a few more winters."

*This original painting by Eleanor Peardis of Seattle, Washington, was made from a recently discovered photograph on a very old post card. The Duwamish Chief holds a hat of fine basketry, beautifully decorated in design typical of the area. Photo: Bureau of Indian Affairs.*

Seattle was the first signer of the Port Elliott Treaty of 1855 which placed Washington tribes on reservations.

But in the wake of the new treaties, several Indian groups, placed on reservation lands which did not include hunting or fishing areas, opened attack on white settlers. "Horse" tribes of eastern Washington combined to lead a war in which they tried to enlist "canoe" Indians. Some coastal tribes did join the alliance, but Seattle's followers remained generally loyal to whites and were evacuated in sloops and canoes to Port Madison Reservation. Throughout this and other Indian wars of the period, Seattle faithfully supported the white cause, at the same time continuing to be a true and powerful leader of his own people.

In line with the tribal belief that mention of a dead man's name disturbs his spirit, Seattle levied a small tribute in advance upon the citizens of the new town named after him. At about 86, he died on Port Madison Reservation.

An Indian burial ground at Suquamish, Wash., 14 miles from Seattle, contains the grave of the great chief. A granite shaft erected there by the people of Seattle is inscribed: "Seattle, Chief of the Suquamish and Allied tribes, died June 7, 1866, the firm friend of the Whites, and for him the City of Seattle was named by its founders." Each year the grave is the scene of a memorial ceremony conducted by local Boy Scouts on Scout Anniversary Day. In Seattle itself, a bronze statute represents the Indian leader in a typical pose, his hand outstretched in a gesture of perpetual peace and friendship.

# RED CLOUD (Oglala Sioux)

"A MAGNIFICENT SPECIMEN physical manhood, as full of action as a tiger."

So Mahpiua Luta ("Red Cloud," from a meteor which turned the sky scarlet at the time of his birth), was described by famed Indian fighter Gen. George Crook, as the Oglala Sioux chief, then 44, led Indian opposition to Government proposals to construct forts along the Bozeman Trail in 1865.

No white encroachment was more bitterly resented by the Teton, or Western Sioux, and the Cheyennes than this attempt to fortify the wild road across the western part of the continent through Wyoming to the newly discovered gold fields of Montana, for the Bozeman Trail cut across the best remaining buffalo grounds.

The Indians had a powerful voice of opposition in Red Cloud. One of the principal chiefs of the Oglala Teton Sioux, he was a foremost warrior who had counted a large number of coups (separate deeds of bravery in battle), a natural leader who had become spokesman for his people through his own force of character. He was in his own right chief of the powerful Bad Face band of Oglalas, and influenced most of the other Oglala Sioux bands.

Red Cloud was grimly determined to keep the Army out of Indian hunting grounds. With a party of Sioux and Cheyennes, he intercepted the first small detachment of troops sent out to begin constructions along the Bozeman Trail in the summer of 1865, and kept them prisoner for more than 2 weeks. When commissioners were sent to treat with the Sioux that fall, Red Cloud refused to allow transactions to start, and himself boycotted the council.

The following June, white negotiators again attempted to get Sioux and Cheyenne permission for passage of emigrants and construction of forts along the trail. This time, Red Cloud was present as a leading representative for the Indians. With great force and dignity, he repeated his refusal to endanger the hunting grounds of his people: the Great Spirit had told him, he said, what would happen to the Indians if the Bozeman Trail became a major route.

But even while discussions were taking place, a strong force of troops had arrived and begun occupation of Wyoming's Powder River country. Upon learning this the furious Red Cloud seized his rifle, shouted a defiant message, and stalked out of the meeting tent with his followers.

The Army proceeded to carry out orders to fortify the trail. When Red Cloud's protests were ignored, he organized his forces, threatened death to any whites who ventured onto the trail, and began a constant harassment which was to go on for 2 years and become known as "Red Cloud's War." The largest post on the trail, Fort Phil Kearny, was kept under relentless sedge, and not even a load of hay could be brought in from the prairies except under strongly armed guard. When Capt. William J. Fetterman, with 80 men, attempted to rescue a woodcutting party under attack near the fort in December 1866, Red Cloud's warriors lured them into ambush and killed every one.

Although there were some white victories, Red Cloud and his followers resisted so effectively that again the Government attempted to negotiate. The new meeting was called for November 1868. Red Cloud's ultimatum was complete abandonment of all posts and of all further attempt to open the Montana road. He refused to sign—or even be present—until the garrisons had actually been withdrawn and he had seen the hated forts burn to the ground.

*Although dressed in full regalia, Red Cloud, the Oglala Sioux warrior, aged and almost blind, had made his home on Pine Ridge Reservation in South Dakota for many years at the time this picture was made. Photo: Smithsonian Institution.*

Red Cloud's victory was complete. The Oglala chief stands alone in the history of the American West as the chief who won a war with the United States.

Having signed the Fort Laramie Treaty, which created the vast area known as the Great Sioux Reservation, he agreed to lay down his arms and settle at Red Cloud Agency in Nebraska. He kept his promise to live peacefully, but not without cost: his acceptance of reservation life brought him the scorn of Crazy Horse and other Oglala leaders, who continued to fight the whites. Red Cloud took no active part in the Sioux hostilities of the 1870's, although many of his followers, and his own son, left the agency to join Sitting Bull and other Sioux warriors.

In 1878, Red Cloud moved his people to Pine Ridge Agency, along with almost all other Oglalas. There, his running feud with Agent McGillicuddy became legendary, primarily because of the agent's persistent efforts to rob him of his prestige and authority as chief of his people. While he advocated peace, Red Cloud was opposed to efforts to rush Indian acceptance of white men's ways, and was a persistent critic of the Federal Government. He left the house built for him by the Government on Pine Ridge to travel to Washington on several occasions, and his views became known to newspaper readers throughout the country.

A few years before his death, Red Cloud and his wife were formally baptized as Roman Catholics; he took the baptismal name "John," and she became "Mary." In 1909, having become feeble and totally blind, the old warrior died in his Pine Ridge home. A marker locates his grave at the Holy Rosary Mission near Pine Ridge Agency, South Dakota.

# CUSTER'S LAST STAND
## *Indian Day of Glory*

This remarkable pictograph, the original painted on muslin, illustrates in true Indian fashion the Battle of the Little Bighorn, Mont., on June 25, 1876, in which Gen. George A. Custer was killed and his command annihilated by combined forces of Sioux and Cheyenne Indians. The Sioux artist was Kicking Bear, a survivor, who painted his recollection of the battle at Pine Ridge, S. Dak. in 1898, 22 years after the Sioux' greatest victory.

The four standing figures in the central group are, left to right: Sitting Bull, Rain-in-the-Face, Crazy Horse, and Kicking Bear himself. The space next to Kicking Bear shows that Chief Gall was deliberately omitted, since he later joined the reconciled Sioux, whereas Sitting Bull and Kicking Bear remained forever hostile to the whites.

The slain Custer (whom the Indians called "Long Hair"), is shown, left, wearing his favorite buckskin costume. Outlined figures at top left represent spirits escaping from the bodies of dead and dying soldiers, while, at the extreme left margin, bursts of gunfire are still coming from Indian guns. At lower right, women in Indian village are beginning Victory Chant; even the dogs join in celebrating. One Indian woman displays a captured American flag.

# CRAZY HORSE (Oglala Sioux)

CRAZY HORSE (TASHUNKE WITKO) a military figure of the Oglala Sioux tribe, came to power while still a young man in his middle twenties, during Red Cloud's War along the Bozeman Trail.

Unlike Red Cloud, Crazy Horse did not settle on Sioux lands established by the 1868 Fort Laramie Treaty, but with his followers, stayed out in the unceded buffalo country to the west.

Courageous, daring, skilled in the techniques of Indian warfare, the bold and implacable Crazy Horse never yielded in his hatred of the white man, and made it clear that he had no intention of abandoning hunting and fighting for reservation existence.

In December of 1875, the Indian Commissioner in Washington, alarmed by reports of Sioux hostilities, directed that all Indians in the area return to their agencies by January 31, 1876. When some Sioux bands, far afield in search of game, failed to meet this impossible deadline, Gen. George Crook was ordered to attack their winter settlements, and he sent Col. J. J. Reynolds to take Crazy Horse's village by surprise. Crazy Horse organized a counter-attack, recovered his warriors' scattered ponies, and drove off Crook's cattle. Without food, the General was forced to return with his men to his post.

Realizing that Crazy Horse was a more formidable adversary than he had thought, Crook planned a new strategy, and the following June, with 15 troops of cavalry and 5 of infantry, marched up the Bozeman Trail to the Tongue River. On June 17, his army ran headlong into 1,200 Oglalas and Cheyennes under Crazy Horse at the Rosebud River. At the end of a day-long battle, Crook was forced to withdraw with heavy losses, chagrined at his second defeat at the hands of the Sioux chief.

A week later, Gen. George A. Custer attacked the fugitive village where more than 3,000 Indian warriors were encamped along Montana's Little Big Horn River. Again Crazy Horse played a leading role. After the repulse of Maj. Marcus A. Reno's battalion by Indians under Sitting Bull and other chiefs, the braves concentrated almost their entire force on Custer and his men, some 4 miles away. In little more than an hour, the Sioux and Cheyennes had overrun Custer and his 224 men, slaughtering every one.

After their victory at the Battle of the Little Big Horn ("Custer's Last Stand"), the Indian bands dispersed. One by one, as more and more soldiers poured into their country, they surrendered.

In January of 1877, Gen. Nelson A. Miles, surprising Crazy Horse's winter camp, scattered the Indians without food or adequate clothing on the frozen plain. The following May, Crazy Horse and about 1,000 men, women, and children surrendered to the Sioux Chief's old adversary, General Crook, at Red Cloud Agency in Nebraska.

But the young warrior could not stand reservation life. Rumors flew that he was plotting escape, and on September 5, 1877, he was placed under arrest. When he realized that he was about to be locked up, Crazy Horse, desperate, drew his knife and tried to cut his way to freedom. He was bayoneted in the back by a white sentry, and died several hours later.

When the Oglalas left the Red Cloud Agency, Crazy Horse's remains went with them to Pine Ridge Agency. Legend has it that they were subsequently moved from their original burial place there, and given a final resting place near a spectacular butte close to Manderson, S. Dak., known as "Crazy Horse Butte."

No photograph has ever certainly been identified as that of the great Sioux warrior, although pictures of other Sioux who resembled him somewhat, have sometimes been claimed to be his.

# SITTING BULL
# (Hunkpapa Sioux)

TATANKA IYOTAKE (SITTING BULL), known the world over as Sitting Bull, the most famous chief of the Teton or Western Sioux, today still ranks as the Sioux of Sioux. The acknowledged leader of history's largest assembly of Plains warriors, a band chief in his own right, a shaman and a visionary with extraordinary ability to plan and organize, he exemplified in every respect the highest Sioux virtues of courage, generosity, and steadfast loyalty to tribal ideals.

Sitting Bull was born in what is now South Dakota about 1831, the son of a Hunkpapa Teton generally known as Jumping Bull. He was scarcely 10 years old when he went on his first buffalo hunt, and at 14, with a war party against Crow Indians, counted his first coup (a war honor involving the touching or striking of a living enemy). As a result of this great feat, his boyhood name— "Slow"—was formally changed to Sitting Bull. Sitting Bull told much of the story of his own life in a series of pictures, and this brave deed is the first of some 63 exploits preserved in his autobiographical drawings.

The Sioux chief believed that he had been divinely chosen to lead and protect his people, and established himself in this role while still a young man. A Crow bullet lamed him permanently when he was in his early thirty's, but did not succeed in limiting his activities. Sitting Bull was on the warpath with his followers almost continuously in the years after 1866, and although other tribes of the northern Plains increasingly resigned themselves to reservation life, he remained with his people in the buffalo country, aloof, uncompromising, and quick to challenge white invaders.

In December of 1875, the Commissioner of Indian Affairs directed all Sioux bands to come onto reservations by the end of January, or be declared hostile. Unable to meet this unrealistic deadline, Crazy Horse and his camp were attacked by troops under General Crook. The Indians dispersed, and Crazy Horse and his people eventually made their way to Sitting Bull's camp on the Rosebud River in the Valley of the Little Big Horn.

By the spring of 1876, around 3,000 Teton Sioux and Northern Cheyenne warriors had assembled at Sitting Bull's camp and had chosen him as their supreme commander. Although few whites then realized the strength of his army, the efficiency of his braves was well recognized. The Sioux, said Gen. Frederick W. Benteen, an Army officer of the time, were

*Tatanka Iyotake (Sitting Bull), the great Hunkpapa Sioux chief was about 51 years old at the time this picture was made at his home on Standing Rock Reservation in North Dakota. Photo: Smithsonian Institution.*

"good shots, good riders, and the best fighters the sun ever shown on."

Sitting Bull, whose insight and political judgment were as remarkable as his military skill, realized that the Sioux and other Plains tribes were about to face a battle for their very existence. In June of 1876, he vowed to perform the Sun Dance, which would give him a vision of what lay ahead for his people. He had often performed this dance, the Plains Indians' greatest and most important religious ceremony, and his chest and back were scarred by its torture.

For this great Dance, Sitting Bull gave 100 pieces of skin from his arms and shoulders. Then, bleeding heavily, he danced all of one day and night. Around noon the next day, becoming almost unconscious, he had the vision for which he had prayed: many white soldiers, falling upside down from the sky, would make war upon his people, but the Great Spirit would care for his Indians.

Sitting Bull's vision was quickly fulfilled. On June 16, more than 1,000 warriors under Crazy Horse met Gen. George Crook and 1,300 armed men at the Battle of the Rosebud. Although tired from the Sun Dance, Sitting Bull was there to urge the Indians on. At the end of an all-day fight, Crook was forced to retreat, with heavy losses.

Despite this victory, Sitting Bull knew that his vision had not yet been fulfilled, for it had showed him many white soldiers. The battle which followed on June 25 was the spectacular Indian triumph known as "Custer's Last Stand," in which the General and every one of his 224 men were annihilated.

No trap had been laid for Custer and his forces, and no strategy planned ahead of time. The battle was a sudden defensive action.

The hostile Sioux and Cheyenne were constantly harrassed by troops under Col. Nelson A. Miles after the Battle of the Little Big Horn, and in the winter following their great victory, many of Sitting Bull's followers surrendered. Pursued by the Army, failing in his attempt to prevent the loss of hunting grounds in the Black Hills and Powder River country, Sitting Bull and his followers escaped to Canada.

Across the border, Sitting Bull pled with Canadians for a reservation, but without success. U.S. commissioners came to Canada to persuade him to return. Sitting Bull resisted, but when there was nothing left to eat, he led his followers south, and surrendered at Fort Buford, Mont., on July 19, 1881. Horses and arms were relinquished in exchange for a "pardon" for Sitting Bull's past.

For 2 years, the Sioux chief was a prisoner of war at Fort Randall. He had become a legend in his own time, and was deluged by fan mail. Lt. Col. G. P.

Ahern, who handled Sitting Bull's letters, described him even then as "a very remarkable man—such a vivid personality... squared-shouldered, deep-chested, a fine head, and the manner of a man who knew his ground. For several months I was in daily contact with Sitting Bull and learned to admire him for his many fine qualities."

Placed on Standing Rock Reservation in 1883, Sitting Bull continued to regard himself as chief of his people. In doing so, he aroused the animosity and jealousy both of Agent James McLaughlin and of rival chiefs. For a year, the venerable chief went on tour with Buffalo Bill's wild west show, but most of the 1880's were spent feuding with McLaughlin.

When the Ghost Dance movement hit Dakota reservations in 1890, tensions between McLaughlin and Sitting Bull were accented. The Sioux chief had endorsed—although without enthusiasm—the new Indian religious movement, and in December of that year had been invited to visit Pine Ridge Agency "to greet the Messiah." McLaughlin used his request for a pass as a pretext that Sitting Bull planned to flee the reservation, and on December 15 sent a detachment of Indian police to arrest him.

Some of his faithful friends tried to prevent Sitting Bull's seizure but during the struggle he was killed by Sergeants Red Tomahawk and Bullhead. His 17-year-old son and six others also died in the skirmish.

Sitting Bull was buried in the Post Cemetery at Fort Yates, North Dakota. In 1953, 63 years after his death, his remains were exhumed and transferred across the Missouri River to Mobridge, South Dakota. A granite shaft marks the last resting place of the great Sioux chief.

# WOVOKA (Paiute)

IN 1888, A YOUNG Northern Paiute Indian named Wovoka, seriously ill with a fever during a total eclipse of the sun, had a vision. Recovering, he told of a revelation from the Great Spirit.

"When the sun died I went up to Heaven and saw God and all the people who had died a long time ago," he reported to his tribesmen. "God told me to come back and tell my people they must be good and love one another, and not fight, or steal, or lie.

"He gave me this dance to give my people."

Wovoka's message began a cult known as the Ghost Dance, which was to spread among Indian tribes from the Missouri River to the Rocky Mountains and beyond.

A medicine man and dreamer whose father, Tavibo, had also been a medicine man, Wovoka was born around 1858 in Mason Valley, Nev. When Tavibo died, the 14-year-old Wovoka was taken into the family of a local rancher, David Wilson, as a farmhand, and given the name "Jack Wilson," by which he became generally known. The spiritual leanings Wovoka inherited from his father were enhanced by the Wilsons' practice of reading the Bible aloud, and the young Indian boy was strongly impressed by accounts of Jesus and His miracles.

Wovoka did not claim divinity after his vision, but quickly became accepted among Indians as the Messiah who would carry the Great Spirit's message. His doctrine, an explicitly peaceful one, promised that Indian lands would be restored; that Indian dead would arise; and that buffalo, deer, elk, and other game would once again roam the plains in abundance. All Indians would be saved by dancing the sacred Ghost Dance.

The first major performance took place near Wovoka's home in early 1889. Visitors to subsequent ones from dozens of western tribes became eager disciples who carried the Ghost Dance far beyond Nevada.

The dance was an extremely simple one, in which for 5 consecutive nights, participants joined hands in a circle and shuffled slowly to the left, while chanting especially composed songs of hope and delivery. Dancers usually wore shirts (often of Government-issue muslin) painted with mystic designs which some tribes believed would be proof against the white man's bullets.

Wovoka's message was perfectly timed for special appeal to western Indians. Plains tribes, confined to reservations, unable to hunt their own food or practice the traditional Sun Dance which for countless years had been their source of spiritual help, took up the Messiah cult and sometimes danced until they collapsed. Among its most enthusiastic followers were the Sioux, who by 1889 were dancing near several South Dakota agencies. Troops were sent in for the protection of apprehensive settlers who feared the new ceremony as a preparation for war.

In December of 1890, about 500 men of the 7th Cavalry (Custer's old regiment) were sent to round up a party of Miniconjou Sioux from Cheyenne River Agency. The party pitched camp at Wounded Knee Creek, about 25 miles from Pine Ridge Agency.

On December 29, having surrounded the Indians, a battery of guns trained upon their tipis, soldiers began to disarm Sioux warriors. During the search for concealed weapons a gun was fired, probably by one of the Sioux. It may have been a signal, for at once other braves threw off their blankets and attacked. White soldiers immediately responded with deadly gunfire.

*This charcoal drawing of Wovoka (Jack Wilson), the Paiute "Messiah", was made from a photograph by James Mooney, a great early student of Indian cultures. Photo: Smithsonian Institution.*

Within half an hour almost all the Sioux warriors had been slaughtered; then guns were turned on the Indian women and children, mowing them down in flight. About 25 soldiers, and more than 200 Indians lost their lives in the dreadful Massacre of Wounded Knee, which ended, for all time, Sioux armed resistance to whites.

Wovoka was dismayed by news of Wounded Knee, since his message had never counseled bloodshed. Although his messianic doctrine persisted for a decade after Wounded Knee, he altered his prophecies as the years went by, and repeatedly called upon his people to follow the white man's road. In 1926, Col. Tim McCoy, then a star of motion pictures and wild west shows, and a friend of the American Indian, went to visit the old prophet. "I found a man unusually vigorous for nearly 70," McCoy said. "He talked readily of the ghost dance religion, and still declared he had visited and talked to God."

Wovoka died quietly in 1932, and was buried in the Indian graveyard at Mason Valley, Nevada.

# JOSEPH (Nez Perce)

FOR CENTURIES, THE Nez Perce (Pierced Nose, a name given these Indians by French trappers because some tribal members once wore shell ornaments in their noses), ranged the grassy hills and plateaus where present boundaries of Washington, Idaho, and Oregon meet. They were a strong, intelligent, and populous people whose traditional friendship to whites was established as early as 1805 with the coming of Lewis and Clark.

The tribe gave up most of its gathering territory to the United States under an 1855 treaty, and settled on designated lands in Oregon and Idaho. Its most powerful band, occupying ancestral lands in Oregon's fertile Wallowa Valley, was led by Chief Joseph, a Christian convert and the lifelong friend of white missionaries, settlers, and explorers.

The old chief's eldest son, born around 1840 as Hinmaton-yalatkit (referring to "thunder coming up over the land from the water"), has become famous as Chief Joseph. He was made the band's leader while still a young man, not through prowess as a warrior or hunter, but because of his superior intelligence and remarkable strength of character.

When gold was discovered on Nez Perce Oregon lands in 1863, and prospectors swarmed into tribal territory, the Indians demanded that their rights under the 1855 treaty be enforced. In response, Nez Perce bands were called together by Indian commissioners in an attempt to persuade the tribe to "adjust" reservation boundaries to an area of less than one-fourth the original.

Failing to reach unanimous agreement, the tribe split into factions and disbanded. Joseph, and several other Nez Perce chiefs,

*Chief Joseph. This photo of the Nez Perce hero is believed to have been made shortly after his surrender and classic speech to the U.S. Army in 1877. Photo: Smithsonian Institution.*

55

would have no part of the treaty, but one leader, Lawyer, tempted by its promises of cash and other benefits, accepted and signed the treaty. The Nez Perce chief had no intention of betraying the rest of the tribe, believing that bands which had not signed would not be bound by his signature. White authorities, however, held that Lawyer's action committed all Nez Perce bands.

Joseph and his followers continued to occupy the Wallowa Valley, and for a time they were left in relative peace. But old Joseph, nearing death, looked into the future and warned his son.

"When I am gone," he counseled the young chief, "think of your country. You are the chief of these people. They look to you to guide them. A few more years and the whites will be all around you. They have their eyes on this land. My son, never forget my dying words: never sell the bones of your father and mother."

No sooner had old Joseph died than the Wallowa was opened to homesteaders, and pressure to remove the Nez Perce began. With dignity and courtesy, but with inflexible determination unchanged by orders or threats, Joseph refused to be moved. "I believe the (1863) treaty has never been correctly reported," he said. "If we ever owned the land we own it still, for we never sold it."

The Wallowa became the subject of a series of conflicting and confusing decrees. In an Executive Order of 1873, the northern part of their own land was returned to the Nez Perce, but 2 years later the order was rescinded and the valley again declared open to homesteading. Joseph counseled his people to be patient, moved their camps from settlers' vicinities, and again appealed to Federal authorities. In 1877 he was given an ultimatum: all Nez Perce must leave within 30 days or be forcibly removed by the Army.

Forced to abandon his father's counsel, and opposing members of the band who advocated war rather than removal, Joseph undertook the sad task of persuading his people to leave the Wallowa. As the allotted time drew to an end, a group of angry Nez Perce killed several whites. Troops sent to the area were all but annihilated by Joseph's warriors in the Battle of White Bird Canyon. In subsequent battles, the Indians continued to outmaneuver white soldiers.

As Nez Perce leader and chief spokesman in opposing the treaty, Joseph was assumed, by whites, to be the band's military genius as well. Although he sat in councils and guided his people's decisions, Joseph was not a war chief; the band's battle victories had been under such chiefs as Five Wounds, Toohoolhoolzote, Looking Glass, and others. But the Army was unaware of this, and Joseph's fame grew to legendary proportions.

In 1877, Gen. O. O. Howard and 600 men, sent to capture Joseph, fought a 2-day battle with Nez Perce warriors near Kamiah, Idaho. Rather than surrender, Joseph chose a retreat that ranks among the most masterly in U.S. military history.

Heading for the Canadian border, he led some 750 followers across four States, twice across the Rockies, through what is now Yellowstone Park, and across the Missouri River, a journey of more than 1,500 miles. Joseph himself took charge of the band's women, children, aged, and ill, while his brother Ollokot and other war chiefs twice fought and defeated white soldiers along the way.

On October 5, 1877, within about 30 miles of the Canadian border, the band was cut off by fresh troops, and Joseph was forced to admit defeat.

His surrender speech, recorded by General Howard's adjutant, has gone down in history as the symbol of Nez Perce dignity and courage:

"Tell General Howard I know his heart. What he told me before I have in my heart. I am tired of fighting. Our chiefs are killed. Looking Glass is dead. Toohoolhoolzote is dead. The old men are all dead. It is the young men who say yes and no. He who led the young men is dead. It is cold and we have no blankets. The little children are freezing to death. My people, some of them, have run away to the hills, and have no blankets; no food; no one knows where they are, perhaps freezing to death. I want to have time to look for my children and see how many I can find. Maybe I shall find them among the dead.

"Hear me, my chiefs. I am tired. My heart is sick and sad. From where the sun now stands, I will fight no more forever."

In 1885, after several years in Indian Territory (Oklahoma), Joseph and most of his followers were sent to Colville Reservation in Washington, where he died in 1904, still an exile from his beloved valley.

*Quanah Parker, from an 1892 photo made when the Comanche leader was about 57 years old. Photo: Smithsonian Institution.*

# QUANAH PARKER (Comanche)

FOR MANY YEARS the word "Comanche" meant terror on the Texas frontier. In early 19th century, Comanche Indians had been generally friendly to Americans, but they became bitter enemies of the Texas settlers who took over their best buffalo hunting grounds.

Wildest and fiercest of Comanches was the Kwahadi band. In 1835, Kwahadis attacked a small settlement in east Texas and carried away several captives, among them a little girl, Cynthia Ann Parker, then about 10 years old. Cynthia grew up to marry Nokoni, a Comanche chief. Their oldest son, born about 1845, was Quanah Parker, who, in Comanche tradition, was given his mother's surname.

Quanah grew up with the savage Kwahadi Comanches, and when his father died, he became the tribe's new chief, a tribute to the young man's ability and intelligence, since chieftainships were not ordinarily inherited among the Comanches.

Fights with the Comanches were an almost everyday occurrence to settlers on the plains of west Texas, and Indian attacks on travelers were a constant danger. The 1867 Medicine Lodge Treaty had assigned Comanches, Kiowas, Kiowa-Apaches, Cheyennes, and Arapahoes to reservations. But Parker and his band, who had refused to sign, continued to hunt buffalo on the Plains and to plunder settlements along the Texas border.

In the early 1870's, when white hunters illegally invaded Indian country and slaughtered vast numbers of buffalos to collect hides, Parker's fury reached its peak. Having mustered about 700 warriors from among the Comanches, Cheyennes, and Kiowas, in June of 1874 he attacked the post at Adobe Walls, where some 30 buffalo hunters were quartered. But the fort's thick walls and superior ammunition were too much for the Indian braves, who were forced to withdraw with severe losses after 3 days of heavy fighting.

Most Comanche aggression came to an end when U.S. Army troops were sent into Indian country. Parker, however, continued to remain on the Staked Plains with his band until the summer of 1875, when he surrendered.

As other leaders before him, Parker had dreamed of an alliance—this time of Plains Indian tribes— which would be strong enough to resist the inroads of white settlement. Once having surrendered his dream, however, he changed his point of view completely, and resolved to adjust to the dominant civilization. "I can learn the white man's ways," he said, and he did.

Parker was still young, and his real career, which was to be long and distinguished, started at that point. He influenced even the wildest of the

Comanche bands to come onto southwestern Oklahoma reservations, and peace at last came to the Texas plains.

For the next 30 years, Parker acted as the industrious and able leader of a confederation of Comanches, Apaches, and Kiowas. He was their most able and influential businessman, and their guide to white civilization. The once-savage warrior made education popular, encouraged homebuilding and agriculture, and initiated the leasing of surplus pasture lands for Indian income. Always, however, he held fast to traditionally important Indian beliefs and ceremonies. Quanah's involvement with the Peyote Cult (peyote is a small cactus whose "buttons," when chewed, produce visions), played an important part in his ability to influence his followers. Parker had five wives (polygamy was customary among the Comanches), and many children, all of whom were educated. He spoke both English and Spanish fluently, and traveled frequently to Washington.

Quanah Parker, the most esteemed Indian of his tribe, died in 1911, at about 76. In 1957, he was reburied in the post cemetery at Fort Sill, Oklahoma., with military honors.

# GERONIMO (Apache)

WITH THE PIERCING shout of Geronimo, U.S. paratroopers plummet from their troop-carrying aircraft. The cry recalls the fiery spirit of the last and most feared of Apache war leaders.          Geronimo fought beside Cochise, Victorio, and Mangas Coloradas, but long after these bold chieftains had passed from the scene his name spread panic in the frontier settlements of the Southwest.

One after another, in the 1860's and 1870's, the Apache tribes capitulated to the advancing frontier, abandoned their raiding forays into Mexico, and allowed themselves to be concentrated on reservations. Among the last to succumb were the Chiricahua Apaches. These were Geronimo's people. Although not born a Chiricahua, he had married a Chiricahua woman and gained stature in the tribe as a warrior of note. A short, thick-set man with a perpetual scowl, he bore the unlikely name of Goyathlay—One Who Yawns—but to his white enemies he was known as Geronimo. By 1876 he was in his middle forties.

In this year the Government removed the Chiricahuas from their mountain homeland in southeastern Arizona. Geronimo rose to leadership of rebellious tribesmen who wanted no part of farming on the parched bottomlands of the San Carlos Reservation. For the next decade he and a small band of "renegades" alternately raided in Arizona and Mexico and grudgingly accepted reservation restraints at San Carlos.

In the autumn of 1881, Geronimo and other leaders once more bolted the reservation and took refuge in Mexico. From strongholds in the rugged Sierra Madre they ranged through the settlements of Mexico and southern Arizona, plundering, burning, and killing. The U.S. Army sent Gen. George Crook to Arizona. An experienced Indian fighter who believed that only Apaches could catch Apaches, Crook enlisted Chiricahua scout units and plunged into Mexico. Persistent pressure, allowing the hostiles no security, finally brought about their return to San Carlos in 1883 and 1884.

But in 1885 Geronimo fled again with a following of less than 50 warriors, and their families. Again Crook put columns into Mexico. Again, in the spring of 1886, Geronimo surrendered to Crook. But this time, fired with intoxicating mescal obtained from a white trader, he dashed for his mountain refuge before even crossing the border.

Stung by criticism from his superiors, Crook asked to be relieved. Gen. Nelson A. Miles took his place, and throughout the summer of 1886 his troops hunted Geronimo and his people in the Mexican wilderness. At last

*Geronimo. The Apache war chief's legendary ferocity is clearly portrayed in this rare photograph by A. Frank Randall, made in 1886. Photo: Smithsonian Institution.*

Lt. Charles B. Gatewood succeeded in getting into Geronimo's camp and persuading him to give up. With him at the last were less than two dozen warriors and their families.

This time the Army took no chances. A military band played "Auld Lang Syne" on the parade ground of Fort Bowie as Geronimo and the last of the Apache hostiles were loaded on wagons to be taken to the railroad and deported from their Arizona homeland.

Nearly all the Chiricahuas—those who had remained peacefully at San Carlos as well as the hostiles and, cruelly, Crook's former scouts too—were imprisoned first in Florida, then in Alabama, and finally in Oklahoma. Resigned to the inevitable, Geronimo allowed himself to be exhibited at expositions in St. Louis and Omaha and even rode in President Theodore Roosevelt's inaugural parade in 1905. He embraced Christianity, affected a stovepipe hat, and once was photographed behind the steering wheel of an automobile. Pneumonia finally took his life at the Fort Sill hospital in 1909. Some of Geronimo's followers may still be found at Fort Sill, Oklahoma., and on the Mescalero Apache Reservation in New Mexico.